Sirens and Seriemas:

Photographs and Poems of the Amazon and Pantanal

Paul Brooke

Brambleby Books

Sirens and Siriemas: Photographs and Poems of the Amazon and Pantanal

Text and photographs © Paul Brooke 2015

The author has asserted his right
under the Copyright, Designs and Patents Act 1988
to be identified as the Author of this Work.

All Rights Reserved

No part of this book may be reproduced in any form
by photocopying or by any electronic or mechanical means,
including information, storage or retrieval systems,
without permission in writing from both the copyright
owner and the publisher of this book.

A CIP catalogue record for this book is
available from the British Library

ISBN 978 1908241 368

First published in 2015 by
BRAMBLEBY BOOKS
www.bramblebybooks.co.uk

Cover design by
Tanya Warren – Creatix Design Services
Cover image by Paul Brooke

Printed by Lightning Source

Sirens and Seriemas:

Photographs and Poems of the Amazon and Pantanal

Acknowledgments

Thanks to Grand View University for granting me a sabbatical, which gave me the opportunity to travel to Brazil and create this book.

Deep appreciation to my skilled Brazilian guides and traveling companions: Eduardo Cunha with Amazon Tree Climbing, Eduardo Sulinski de Campos and Anselma at Uakari Lodge, Eduardo Coelho, John at Pantanal Wildlife Center, and Ricardo Casarin at the Chapada dos Guimarães.

Special gratitude to Estéfani Fujuti at the Projeto Boto in the Mimirauá Reserve. The project's work on the study of botos and tucuxis, both admirable and necessary. Please visit their website at www.projetoboto.com for more information about the ruthless practice of paracatinga fishing and preservation work on the botos.

Memorable recognition for the hospitality at Caburini and Vila Alencar in the Mamirauá Reserve. They were gracious in letting me get a sense of village life in the Amazon.

Charles Munn designed the trip and waded through the details with me: his insights were invaluable and led me to amazing places.

Extraordinary thanks to Paul Donahue and Teresa Wood, newly found friends, who were incredibly knowledgeable in locating wildlife at the Pantanal Wildlife Center, plus they are just great company! Their stories kept us up late into the night.

Special acknowledgement to the folks at Colrain, who critiqued the manuscript, including Joan Hoalihan, Bill Palmer, Anne Caston, Anne Hasenstab, Kerrin McCadden, Fred Merchant, and Peter Covino.

Finally, thanks to my wife, Corly, who had to endure countless mosquitoes and sometimes primitive conditions in the Pantanal. Her continual support and ethusiasm for nature continue to encourage and improve my work as a photographer and writer!

Introduction

Henry David Thoreau once said, "All good things are wild and free." And Aldo Leopold wrote, "There are some of us who can live without wild things, and some who cannot." I, for one, cannot. I need wild land. I need wild animals. My eye tires of concrete, strip malls, and the sameness of city after city. My heart aches for animals trapped in parks and zoos, the wild draining out of them, the tame defeating them.

When I imagine the wildest places in the world, many locations immediately spring to mind: Africa, Borneo, the Amazon. The Amazon is inextricably linked to the wild for me. As a young boy, I dreamed of visiting and exploring the Amazon. Poetic images emerged of jaguars killing caiman, scarlet macaws nesting high in swollen hollows, and piraracu slapping the surface of the river. I knew if I wanted to truly experience the wild that the Amazon was an ideal starting place.

My first day in the Amazon, outside of Manaus, I visited a family who operated a business of feeding pink river dolphins for tourists. Each day they have two or three feeding times and the botos come readily to the hand to eat fish. The tourists are delighted to see a *wild* dolphin, but I would argue that they are *tame*, not wild. They have been trained to come every day and not hunt in their traditional ways; these practices have altered their behavior.

I came across an advertisement that claimed "near the lodge we have the world's tamest wild tapir." The "tamest wild" phrase struck me and this oxymoron kickstarted the concept for this book. I began to think deeply about the wild and the tame.

The second day in the Amazon I saw my first wild jaguar. It was male (about 80 kilos) and it turned and looked over its shoulder at the three of us (Anselma, Edward S., and me). His rosettes were like black smudges of smoke; his body was muscular and lean. He bolted from the sight of us and literally sprinted away through the flooded forest. Water splashed in a double rhythm. I thought to myself: that was one of the wildest animals I had ever seen.

Wild animals should challenge a photographer. Typically, they are skittish and flee immediately, preserving themselves and their wildness in the process. Perhaps I can get a photograph or two before they leave.

In the Amazon, the golden-backed uakaris are the most challenging animals to photograph. These monkeys, which have evolved specifically to the flooded forest, are active in the highest trees, usually 30 or more meters above the forest floor (in the dry season). Humans make them skittish. I followed the uakaris for eight days straight and once I was 10 meters away from them, but didn't realize it until they fled through the trees at such a blistering pace that I could barely follow them with my eyes. Fortunately, on my last day at Uakari Lodge, I captured shots of one lone uakari feeding right before sunset. There was a satisfaction knowing how diligently I worked to get those images.

My time in the Amazon was transcendental. But my experience in Brazil were far from over; next I was heading to one of the richest places for wildlife in the world: the Pantanal. The fecundity of the Pantanal became evident the moment my wife and I began to travel the Transpantaneira Highway; there was wildlife everywhere: on the road, over the road, next to the road... Capybaras kept cool in the mud of the truck tracks, roadside hawks perched on fenceposts, and jabiru storks feasted in the flooded margins. My camera never left my hand.

At the Pantanal Wildlife Center, a viewing platform has been built directly across from the jabiru storks' nest. At first, I felt enormously guilty photographing them on the nest, but as I realized that if I moved slowly, made little sound, and left quietly, I would make the least impact on them. These birds were somewhat habituated and not completely wild.

At Neco's Camp (a fish camp near Porto Jofre), I was told that the hyacinth macaws were habituated to humans; however, I felt the opposite was true: they were terrified by humans and seemed fearful. If I approached the macaws, they immediately flew far away. So I quietly got up before dawn and waited patiently for them near fruiting palms and was able to successfully photograph them. Their intense blue color was radiant and knocked the breath out of me when the sunlight illuminated them fully. It was inspirational to capture their true essence, their true wildness.

As I spent a month in Brazil, I began to understand how this "tamest wild" concept developed: from a burgeoning ecotourism industry with tourists eager to witness wildlife up close and personal. I, myself, succumbed to the allure of such practices. Within this book I have two photographs from my time with the handfed pink river dolphins. After I talked to Estéfani Fujiti from the Projeto Boto, I understood the way these practices can undermine the health and well being of the animals by introducing them to disease and teaching them the wrong way to hunt, the wrong way to be.

When I was on Lake Mamirauá, I witnessed firsthand the behaviors of truly wild botos (pink dolphins) and tucuxis (grey dolphins) and it was far more exhilarating. They fed, played, and raised their young without human interference. I marveled at their complex social interactions and observed as they worked communely to catch fish. These dolphins were not the "tamest wild", instead they were beautiful creatures living rightly.

This book chronicles my journey to discover the Amazon and the Pantanal, to explore through poetry and photography the complexity of wildlife so abundant there. I had hundreds of transcendental experiences with the wildlife, with the people, and with the natural world. I do not support the "tamest wild", but what I do believe in is the preservation of wild nature.

Paul Brooke

Still, the leaves of dreaming will die
If they are not part of a larger dream
Converted into a tree.

—"A Dream To Tame"
by Thiago de Mello

Contents

Poems:

The Amazon

Before the Amazon	16
Market Catfish	18
Fruit Market	20
Convergence	22
Pink River Dolphins	24
Carrion Fish	26
Black Caiman Under My Bed	28
Opportunist	30
Water Monkey	32
Flat, Dry Ground Prone to Flood	34
Sloth and Moth	36
Terrible Beauty	38
Samauma	40
Gas Bird	42
Lily Trap	44
Isolationist	46
Greater Tinamou	48
Eatable Fear	50
Purest Wild	52
Fishing for Jaguars	54

The Pantanal

Transpantaneira Highway	58
Cemetery for Caimans	60
Table Scraps	62
Alarm Whistle	64
A Charm	66
Drain	68
The Flora of Metaphor	70
Grow Up, Cecropia	72
The Dream of the Hyacinthine	74
Tick, Tick	76
Barren Tree	78
The Magician	80
Naughty	82
Swear-Words	84
Derelict Commune	86
Sirens and Seriemas	88
Junkie of Light	90
Notes	94-96

Photographs:

Anhinga with Catfish	2-3
Grey Dolphin Playing	8
Amazónico Sunset	9
Tiger Heron	12-13
Squirrel Monkey Jumping	14-15
Favelas of Manaus	17
Surubim Catfish at Fish Market	18-19
Date Palm Fruit at Fruit Market	21
Fish Market Before Sunrise	23
Pink River Dolphin	25
Pink River Dolphin Underwater	26-27
Black Caiman	28-29
Gecko on Porch Screen	31
Arawana	32-33
Cipos Flower	35
Brown-Throated Three-Toed Sloth with Moths	37
Tarantula	39
Samauma	40-41
Hoatzin	43
Amazonian Waterlily Blossom	45
Golden-Backed Uakari Monkey	47
Child from Caburini Village	49
Monkey Brush with Ant	51
Jaguar Track	53
Boy with Piranhas	54-55
Two Southern Caracaras at Sunset	56-57
Transpantaneira Highway	59
Black Caiman Claw	61
Black Caiman in Sun	62-63
Young Capybara	65
Female Helmeted Manakin on Nest	67
Sunken Canoe	69
Wattled Jacana on Floating Vegetation	71
Cecropia	72-73
Hyacinth Macaw	75
Lowland Tapir with Ticks	77
Jabiru Storks in Rain	79
Iguana Lounging	81
Capuchin Monkey	83
Greater Rhea	85
Papaya	87
Red-Legged Seriema	89
Illuminated Grasses	90-91
Sunset over the Pantanal	92-93
Black-Bellied Whistling Duck	97

For two inspiring teachers:
Jim Pease and Mary Swander

Before the Amazon
Antes d'Amazon

Papayas thrive wildly in vacant
lots; favelas stack like shifting
decks of cards, many-storied
books, streets oily with rain,
the mind stacks and sorts,
the cat asleep on the pooltable,
the man waking from the couch,
the children's shirts wet
on the clothesline, the woman
in the red dress checking
herself in the glass before work,
beautiful, dislocated,
a bromeliad flower blooming
high in a camu camu.

Market Catfish
Surubim Mercado

Their sides are spray-
painted, graffitied,
big arching
black letters,
balloon,
shape tags,
cartoon characters,
doodles,
nicknames,
riddles,
profanities,
philosophies,
exclamations,
obsessions,
confessions,
their own
bloated
likenesses
swimmming
down the bus stop,
dripping wet paint.

Fruit Market
Mercado Fruta

brazil nuts &
date palms &
one million one million bananas &
guaraná juice &
bacuri fruit &
huge ginger root &
figs &
tucumã &
cacao &
yellow-bruised papayas &
stacked watermelons &
passionfruit in soft bags &
small guavas &
pineapples &
reddish mangoes &

purplish bananas &
plaintains &
starfruit &
cashews in syrup &
dried bananas rolled in sugar &
cinnamon stick to fingers &
tongue lingers, thwacks &
smacks every micron of the sweetmeat &
candied oblivion; sugar rushes blood,
tightens the pupil.
Embrace this release &
this morning heat. Crowds pulse &
flicker; they touchbuy &
touchbuy impulse, impulse,
sweet thing after sweet thing.

Convergence
Convergência

Land-tied briefly, docked
and cocked for departure.

Hard-scrabbled men shovel
the holds of ancient boats.

One captain sags in hammock
wanting well-deserved shuteye.

*Son, stuff each sack with dourada,
arapaima, sardina, and paraiba.*

*Carry on your head to the scales.
Begin with the richest first.*

*Weigh the fish. Haggle well.
Our next two weeks depends.*

*One day this will be yours.
One day you will have a son.*

*Today's the day I entrust you.
Today's the day I stand back.*

*Daughter, mend the nets, sweep
the decks, and sharpen the hooks.*

Pink River Dolphins
Botos

The botos suck air,
take free fish
by the basketfuls.
Charity.

Botos,
secret sharers
of the muddy
Underworld.

Given names.
Stroked like pets.
Propped up.
Conditioned.

Botos,
great battlers,
scarred
Pink.

This isn't love.
It's necessity.
Compulsion.
Rarity.

Botos,
guardians
of the meeting
Waters.

Botos,
holders of rock
and weed.
Desire.

The weak eye
sees, grows wide
with greed.
Knows

when the wild
shrinks
and the tame
Rises.

Carrion Fish
Paracatinga

He had just begun
to believe all
human beings
are inherently good
when he finds the box.

Half-submerged, the box
is baited with a rotting
carcass of a boto. It attracts
a swarm of paracatinga,
the ruthless carrion fish.

Columbians taught
the locals how to build
and prepare the trap.
Most Brazilians do not
even like paracatinga.

Downriver, he finds
a pink dolphin alive,
bound and tied dockside,
surname carved into her flank.
Its baby dead in the shallows.

He cuts the rope and frees her.
She swims under her baby,
tries to elevate it to breathe.
He cannot help but hang
his head in shame.

He doesn't want to accept
the fact: people are pure evil;
they cannot see the cruelty
of their own hands,
their own sick mechanisms.

He climbs the slippery slope
to the fisherman's house,
rope in hand, knife in sheath,
and pounds hard. He thinks,
I am conscience knocking.

"Bring your daughter," he says.
He descends to the dock
and makes the fisherman
watch the mother and the calf.
"Sit," he says, "sit and think."

The daughter nestles into his lap
as the mother nuzzles her dead
calf. Sobbing deep and aching,
the daughter breaks. The father
repeats, "breathe, just breathe."

Black Caiman Under My Bed
Cama por Baixo de Jacaré

Who can sleep? Caimans hunt under the bed, under the floor. Against the floating timbers, they ambush fish.

Slap and gulp them whole. The caiman are dark agents, shadows. Are we pretenders, posers in our own lives?

Açu

Do we swallow enough tinctures
to believe? The fear bubbles up.
Will we be exposed? The caimans
leave us gazing through gauze.

They bang all nightlong,
phantom shapes sliding
through the viscous rivertide,
reminding us of the once was.

They grunt disapproval
of our poor figures and poorer
untruths, ruthless, mouths
laced with blood and bacteria.

We cannot take it anymore
and arise, fire up our headlamps:
uncountable pairs of incandescent
eyes encircle, flicker, and stare.

To caimans, we are hairless
jaguars, overstuffed
monkeys, demons of liquid
sun, parasites of the trees.

Opportunist
Oportunista

To make a sloth descend,
conjure up a harpy eagle.

Form the lips like so.
Blow down, trill a little.

To see a jaguar, check sky.
The vultures smell carrion.

Find the kill and keep alert.
She's lurking, mad and fat.

To catch a piranha, sit
in your dugout, under its tree.

When the caterpillars drop,
use them to bait your hook.

To find a lover, learn forró.
Ask every woman to dance.

When one stays for three
songs, you will get lucky.

To find a lover, learn forró.
Ask every man to dance.

When one stays for a whole
song, you will get lucky.

Water Monkey
Macaco d'Agua

Oh, Arawana,
Greatest Trapeze
Artist of High,

viscous, armored,
enamored
with the sky,

gleaner of flooded
forest, leaper,
beetle cleaner.

Clear the water
farther, shake
and take a bird,

a bat, a moth,
a mouse,
a young sloth.

Grimaced,
laced with blood,
barbed and barbelled,

dusky, eyes
like spinning dishes.
Fins like silky flags.

Tail a machete.
Body a catapult,
tied and set.

Older ancestors
vault vines,
spring from tines.

They are of no
concern. Time to turn
and blur shadow.

Wait for little miscues,
twitches, seizures
on a leaf.

He cascades,
airborne, plucks
and grasps.

Gasp
at the height,
the aerial mastery,

the majesty
of flight,
all without a net.

Flat, Dry Ground Prone to Flood
Restinga

Within weeks, this will all be
covered in a meter of water.
The lower world rushes
to burst into flower, into pollen.
Instinct driving them to panic.

The villagers will hastily build
rafts for their cattle, smaller
ones for their chickens. Float
plants in old canoes near homes,
bring the dogs up to the porches.

The restinga will be overwhelmed.
Seringas and barrigudas harbor
bigger buttresses, trusses and trestles,
where the tambaqui anticipate
the kerplink, kerplunk of seeds.

Restinga turns to cheia, dirt turns
to water, mammal turns to fish…
All of us must redefine what we
now are, adult, parent, elder…
embrace the newfound after grieving.

Sloth and Moth
Preguiça e Traça

Bradipodicola hahneli *lives on the fur of the sloth and lays its eggs when the sloth descends to defecate. About 127 moths can live comfortably on a given sloth. The world's population just reached 7 billion people.*

A bizarre island
drifts slowly, its forests
flowering with algae,

its coastline studded
with spire-sharp
façades of stone,

a peaceful place,
full of grazing
and plenty of naps.

Its inhabitants
live luxuriantly,
not luxuriously,

a gracious host,
ample flesh-pots,
ample panoramas,

a tiny sphere
balanced
in equilibrium.

Terrible Beauty
Beleza Terrível

That which you hate I love:
the forest nocturnal with her
coralsnakes and fer-de-lances,
tarantulas with irritating hairs,
scorpions paralyzed with fear.

That which you hate I love:
trails soupy after rain; mosquitoes
draining and droning; biting ants
on my feet; armadillo wasps
swarming to protect their nest.

That which you hate I love:
scanning for birds with neck
crooked, carrying seventeen kilos
of gear, drinking murky water,
contracting mild diarrhea.

That which you hate I love:
swimming the lake amidst
a cloud of piranhas; swatting
the cockroach from my hammock;
enduring another heat headache.

Think how much more I love
the things I love by loving
the things you hate. I call it
oppositional unity. You laugh
and call it undeniable fate.

Samauma

An ancient woman towers;
bowers of birds and bromeliads
adorn her like pendants.

Her garments are scattered
to netherworlds, taken, given
to the rich, a paltry fortune,

or burned in daily sacrifice
necessity, the hot roast
of manioc, purging water.

Now, she stands impressively,
braced against the sky. A tiny
house laps up her cool shade.

She is safe: the Solimões River
never floods her. Rogue loggers
will never cut, too inconvenient,

too many watchers. Her sisters
are unluckier, deep in the forest,
hidden beauties, sequestered,

banished by their father, soon
to be bed unwillingly by uncouth
suitors, quick buck hucksters.

Gas Bird
Pássaro de Bazófia

Foulest of fowl,
double-stomached
fetid gas bag, gas bird,
decomposer of all leaves.

My dear Hoatzin
quit putting on heirs,
your air is reasty, yeasty,
too putrified for idolatry.

You will never reach
the status of an arapaima,
an araracanga, boto,
or the legend of onça.

Thankfully, your flesh
is tainted, rust-tasting,
ruinous. No one will ever
poach you. Kill for sport.

So sit coffee-klatched
in your low bush, nervous
nellies, crazy old-lady
hairdos, blue eye shadow,

weirdo outfits, mismatched
colors and designs, whispering
gossip about the neighborhood.
Promise to keep your distance.

Lily Trap
Arapuca Lírio

Guarded by a pair
of spiders and a thousand
thorns, the trap isn't
set, but it pauses.

Once revealed, its
appeal is like lit neon
of brilliant purple:
the scarab stumbles

and becomes trapped
in a seedy hotel room,
flouncey bed and pricey
perfume; this night is free.

In morning, he staggers
out of his little boudoir,
nothing to show but
his crumpled clothes.

The light reveals it all,
the aftermath, his drunken
swagger, eyes betraying him,
the hotel room, trashed.

But he never sobers up
and bumbles out, night after
night, onto the cobblestones.
He just can't help himself.

Isolationist
Isolacionista

If I squint,
I see myself
in you.

A face
like a sunburn
tourist's.

A skull,
dull, dented
and draconian.

A coat,
pie-bald,
unwearable in public.

I am vinegar,
no son of Narcissus,
mouth built to crush,

fingers trained
to climb and clamber
through várzea vine,

always scolded, told not
to clamor, not to reveal
my secrets or yours.

Seclusion paralyzes,
takes me to darker
crooks and crannies.

I must decide all:
this shoot, that leaf,
these fruits, that tree.

I am an isolationist
foraging alone
in this superabundance.

Greater Tinamou
Inhambu de Cabeça Vermelha

The high, clear notes
pierce the forest,
unearthly, always
the same distance.
This is true.

The jaguar mimics
the greater tinamou
perfectly, whistling her
to her own doom.
This is untrue.

The village, high on a hill,
floods. Last year, only
five houses were dry; all
families converged, merged.
This is true.

A sucuriju swallowed
a boy whole and the men
slit the snake's skin; the boy
was laid on the porch.
This is untrue.

The children shinny
spindly açais. Money
from the market is good.
One falls now and then.
This is true.

All the children read.
School meets everyday.
There are oodles of books.
Worlds open beyond them.
This is untrue.

Electricity was delivered
by the government, a diesel
generator, lights, television.
The people needed it.
This is true and untrue.

Eatable Fear
Medo Comestíveis

Many fear the jungle,
terrified of everything:
hantavirus, toxoplasmosis,
yellow fever, dengue fever,
schistosomiasis, equinine
encephalitis, cholera,
malaria, candirus,
piranhas, anacondas...

Araçaris pop bacabá
fruits like sweet little pills.
Capuchins gobble flames
of the monkey brushes,
strip bark and lick
the sticky sweetness.
Scarlet macaws hack
the husks from palms.

Nearly everything is edible
in the Amazonian forest:
the skeins of vegetation
floating the river, the sticky
resins gunking up trunks
of trees, tiny ants tasting of
lemon, açaí berries bending
under unbearable weight.

Take a handful and chew.
Hear the forest's texture?
Close your eyes and drink
the sounds like fresh juice.
Hold the flower in hand.

Can you see its sparks?
Yellow and orange, yes.
Fear is eatable, pull
a chair to the table.

Purest Wild
Selvagem Puré

"If prey is vulnerable, jaguars will capitalize."
— *Sandra Cavalcanti*

The young jaguar
is purest wild, not
amenable to givens,
hunting the riverbanks
for whatever he wants.

Briefly, he freezes,
splashes through igapó,
leaving fresh spoor:
forward weight springing
him onto a fallen log.

The old jaguar
is less wild insofar
as he becomes lazy,
makes poor choices, settles
for cattle instead of caiman.

I see him this morning
close to camp. Debating,
it seems, if he should
hunt me. He lingers
in the shade for an hour.

I am that old jaguar, teeth
ground down; I am staying
to the rivers, trying to hunt
only capybaras and dogs, trying
to resist the even easier prey.

But I am not sure I can.
I am weak, my body pockmarked
by scars and puncture wounds,
unseen fractures slowing my gait.
I am ready to break like an old stick.

Fishing for Jaguars
Onça Pesca

Piranhas are gill-
and mouth-tied
to hand lines,
lobbed over
a plane branch,
dangled up down,
up down like
living yo-yos:
tails twitching,
teeth clicking.

Before the jaguar
snatches the bait,
the fish is pulled
into the river.
The men laugh
riotously, "It's like
baiting a drunk
with a five real
on a string. Do it
again. Again."

The jaguar slinks
away into shade;
this scene plays
a thousand times.
Some jaguars act
disinterested,
wander off to drink,
and rush the bait.
Others wait for snags
and easy pickings.

The Pantanal

Transpantaneira Highway

there are not two choices, only one:
the forward slog of gravel crossed
with bog, potholes deep in waterholes,
no chance of sleep, capybaras slurped
in mud, snakes scudding the top
of the tire tracks, five hundred head,
the push to higher ground, pasture,
detering progress, a mass of hooves,
skittish calves and bulls sidestep truck,
hard luck pantaneiros, hats sweatbanded.
it makes a difference to begin early,
to have four-wheel drive, to be an uneager
operator; a believer in downshifting;
in slowing at each bridge, in bringing
extra water, tools, and chains; in helping
those stuck in muck, axle-deep; in telling
jokes in the roughest patches; in idling
often admiring rheas and pampas deer.

Cemetery of the Caimans
Cemitérios Jacaré

During the 1970s, it is estimated one million caimans were killed by coureiros every year.

Retrace poachers' campfires,
kick the charred wood,
the disintegrating drying
racks. They slaughtered masses,
hundreds of thousands
of caiman here. Kneeling,
seek forgiveness for wanton
waste, shoes and handbags,
belts and wallets, skins stretched
taut then rolled tight. Out
scattered in the forest are skulls
and bones, pits and crypts
of the long dead, never honored.
On the river, the night's sky
is a black vestment. The moon
is a new-faced saint. Eyes pulse
the dark margins, hundreds
of thousands of live caiman
rise miraculously from the depths.

Table Scraps
Fragmento

There is no atonement,
reparation for causing
casualty or extinction.

The cook thought no harm,
and so tossed the ham,
catfish, and leg bones.

The guests were startled
by how close the caiman
came, familiarity and name.

They laid down near
the caiman and captured
intimate portraits of its eye.

No one expected so small
a caiman would turn
behemoth, a rogue.

Eat a dog. Terrorize
guests at night by lunging
and snapping jaws.

Shadow and stalk.
Tear flesh from a young
woman's leg like wet paper.

Leave the woman half-
alive, struggling to survive,
clinging to the dock.

There is no atonement,
reparation for causing
casualty or exigency.

The men make a noose
from a rope and ask the cook
to bring more bones.

There is no atonement,
reparation for causing
casualty or extermination.

Alarm Whistle
Assobio Alarme

Capybaras use a series of noises to communicate with each other: whistles, grunts, squeals, and coughs.

When he was small, he rode high
on his father's back to see faces
of the angry crowd. Coaxed
and coached him how to float.
Scampering and freewheeling,
he froze, hearing pai's whistle
carrying across the expanse,
immediately run for home.

When he was old enough, he left
to travel rivers, to stake his claim,
to form his own kinfolk. His was
transitory, distance separated:
he feigned preoccupation and time;
some made miraculous escapes.
He worked diligently to conceal
his weaknesses; hoped no one noticed.

He tried to keep them safe each day,
but they are dragged away, body
by body: they served their purpose.
There was nothing more to do.
He checked downriver searching
for him, ears pricked, intent.
He waited to hear it on the wind:
the clear note of his father's whistle.

A Charm
Amuleto

Helmeted manakins are part of Amazonian superstition and are often killed and used as charms.

Upon finding her on the nest,
name her a living charm,
not hatched in a pocket
or hung dangling from thatch.
Abandon collections,
superstitions, and talisman.
Wish the whole universe
could struggle at first to see,
then lock onto her green
iridescence, and oo and ah.
Whisper so quietly, look
how she's glued the leaves
like little scraps of paper.
Her eye, her eye. Her nest
seems to be a handmade hat.
Or a pistachio ice cream cone.
She's camouflaged so well
no one knows where leaf
ends and bird begins.

Drain
Dreno

Zebu are humped taurines,
lean, grass-guzzling machines
bent on grazing crazily. Skin
flaps, dewlaps sag, and ears
flop; their legs are weird stilts.
Heifers and calves are light-
coated like Charlois. The bulls
are darker grey, horse-dwarfing,
black-hummocked behemoths,
bred for humidity and wading.

To raise well, have pantaneiros
ride alongside; don't damage
their hides with whips; give
them salt licks; drive to fresh
pasture as the rains shift; keep
them high and dry; cut palms
and make pasture; drain the soil
so they won't get stuck or drown;
the more pasture, the more Zebu,
the more pasture, the more Zebu.

The Flora of Metaphor
Flora de Metáfora

*Camalotes are floating beds of
vegetation found in both
the Amazon and Pantanal.*

The jaçaná's feet splay;
he seemingly walks his way
on water like an illusionist,
like Christ. He fishes

poorly like a disciple, tends
his aquatic garden in stilted
heat, deterging and purging
pests, sidestepping perils.

When the banks crest,
the camalotes unanchor,
drift like errant botes,
spun by ebb and eddy.

Underneath, stowaways
latch; above, insects hatch
in the hyacinth scraps and
a cocoi delicately scratches.

At the bend, the floating
islands accumulate, wedge,
and form an impenetrable
mass, a soggy moquette,

a green raft, a lettuce salad,
a Brillo pad, a flat dam, a mat
of uncountable neurons,
an impressionistic painting.

Camalotes are transients,
continents, plate tectonics
shifting with each hour,
each day, faults and rifts

and crevasses forming,
land masses slamming,
advancing and retreating;
meaning slips underfoot.

Grow Up, Cecropia
Cecropia, Crescer-se Adulto

In the dead spaces of terra firma,
the cecropia squats and homesteads,
settles and covets more blank sky,
sends the bulk of its children
across dried allevium to die.

A lucky few grow up and stretch,
gangly as teenagers, awkward with acne.
They rebuke the world. Whorled,
their hands are sticky, haircuts a puzzle,
lives a sprint, a straight line of sight

to the light, no junked up trunk,
always outcompeting peers, shrugging
off any and all distractions, socially
isolated, warming in solar brilliance
inside their own greenhouses.

The Dream of the Hyacinthine
Sonho d'Arara Azul Grande

Nestlings of hyacinth macaws are taken and sold illegally. Only 2500 to 5000 live in the wild today.
— *Charles Munn et al. (1989/1990)*

Nest robbers think macaw feathers
are currency, the young are loot:
they wait for the noisy overhead
rattle clatter of the parents, climb
a jury-rigged ladder, cherrypick
the unfortunate brood, and kidnap
them to some air-picaroon. Wildness matters most in the universe
of the hyacinthine macaws, captivity
makes for impostors, drains color.

Swathed in palm shade, he scratches
field notes in ink: the black eye
marooned by yellow; beak a pair
of tin snips; tip a massive curved
dagger; tongue inlaid with gold;
tail feathers are a tapering mast;
rope-like toes rotate palm nuts;
upper head lighter cobalt; wings
and coverts, intense ultramarine,
a dream of electric blue or of jewels.

Tick, Tick
Tiquetaque, Tiquetaque

Black caracaras, cattle tyrants, shiny cowbirds,
and rufous horneros are tick-eating birds of lowland tapirs.

Most ticks bunker, hunker
under out-of-reach patches,
folds of unscratched skin.

Tiquetaque, tiquetaque,
the tapir rubs and sloughs:
a few ticks burst with blood.

Parasites do not make good
mothers. At dusk, her young
follows the white tips of her ears.

She teaches her stillness
in the broken light, keeps
jaguars and poachers away.

Forays into water, nibbles
of new leaves, plucking ripe
fruit with her flexible trunk,

waddling on the muddy bottom,
breathing with her snorkle,
sniffing the wind for trouble,

allowing tyrants and horneros
to clean, glean, and peck her back,
harvesting, tiquetaque, tiquetaque.

Barren Tree
Árvore Árido

In pantanoso field, the dead tree
is a hand cradling the heavy nest,
mudpacked and waterlogged.

Other couples brave the chuva
torrencial, heavy rains; a chusma
of friends gathers upstairs and down.

Words spoken seem uncertain
and flimsy, a thin curtain separating,
doors and windows varnished shut.

Grief burns in the gut, a pasture's
controlled fire, a hand smacking
the stove's flame, the tumbling

pan, full of hot grease. The pair
is stunned, shellshocked; the pain
heaves and buckles their knees,

hunches and curls their papel wings.
Their silent language drip drips
from beaks, deluges the vacancy.

The Magician
Mágico

His tricks are legendary:
escape from certain death
by flinging himself twenty
meters into a muddy river;
drop a tail and let it squirm
when caught; molt a coat
of arms, sit so green, so
cryptically, so hypnotically
the audience misses him.

The parietal eye notes light
and dark shifts, knows when
a raptor descends, parts clouds,
rips air, and seeks to rend. Now,
threats come from beneath:
collectors with nets and poachers
with rifles. This is his final
trick, his last hurrah. Presto.
Chango. Poof. He disappears.

Naughty
Travesso

Grabbing more than they
should, never listening,

glistening in the dappled
light, capuchins act impishly,

prankishly, like naughty
children given free reign

at the playground. Dropping
sticks, stealing my fruitlunch,

scampering behind, above me,
I whirl and step deep, water

gushing and sloshing boots,
tripping over exposed roots.

The monkeys yap, clap, slap
branches, quickly evaporate.

I am spinning in a tight circle,
laughing hysterically, speaking

to the wind again, scolding
only myself for this foolishness.

Swear-Words
Palavrões

Rheas became curse-words
to farmers, scour-agents,
vacuous-vacuums denuding
field after field after field.

Even before their light eyes
and feathers darkened, they
were chased and harassed
by trucks and shotgun blasts.

Do not deny their appetites:
hectares of seeds, birds, roots,
lizards, legumes, snakes, drupe;
harems of females form flocks.

Males keep sharp-eyed, heads
erect, hair triggers set, legs
cocked like hammers, safeties
unlatched, feathers as silencers,

sky barrel blue, salvoes released,
sharp as shrapnel, these rheas
are ready to fire down the road,
kick up a volley of dirt and debris.

Derelict Commune
Comune Abandonado

Egos and fantasies lead to defeat.
    The commune crumbles to rubble.
Division of labor must feel equal.
    Mangoes are strangled; paths tangle.

Respect nature. Nuture others.
    The papayas rot underfoot.
Resist economic temptations.
    No one can fix the plumbing.

Center on the social family.
    Gils kickboxed and chased women.
Friends, fellowship, and kinship.
    He left to learn from the Xingu.

Each person has gifts to offer.
    Noam carves bongs from burls.
No one is favored over another.
    Clara knows intricate tax law.

Utopia is more than in the mind.
    They offer fresh-blended juice.
Human intellect must be tended.
    Gentle conversation follows.

Mediation and quietness are essentials.
    A porcupine has gnawed the table.
The weak-willed hold others in blame.
    It merely needs a ration of salt.

Sirens and Seriemas
Sereia e Seriemas

On rough-hewn streets,
resist the barker's deal,
the sham artist's steal,
the temptress Siren's lure.

Hurry your way through
stopgap fences and fields,
steer clear of wild swine
reminiscent of old men.

With bloody treats, bribe
a dog like Cerberus, clear
a path to the barbed wire
gate, but this is no Hades.

Take a seat in dry grass.
It isn't long before you see
their long legs, blue eyes.
The seriemas surround.

Daughters of Helios, Perse
strut, pluck snakes, dismiss
forbidden fruits, wear rouge
and crowns of feathers.

Be spellbound by myth,
not by the desire to touch,
to stroke their long necks
and immaculate coats.

Nothing good can come.
Reverse course, withdraw
ever so quietly, and leave
sirens to their vexing ways.

Junkie of Light
Narcotine de Luz Açu

I am a junkie of light:
waking in the thrum
of night, strung out,
jittery, teetering
between reality
and crazed dream.
Stumbling stairs
to the toilet, I need
a fix, an ounce,
a dose, climbing me
to a high, veins
seething, heart
reeling, mouth awry.

I know what to do:
drive past spent spots,
past burned-out lots,
hovels, and fazendas,
into deeper pieces
of cloth, secluded
places, clean swamps.
I was born to shoot up
the wild-eyed dawn,
her light hypnotic,
diffuse, a psychedelic,
an hallucinogenic,
an opiate, an ecstasy.

Notes

"Before the Amazon." The camu camu trees are quite common and produce red and yellow fruits that are very delicious. When the camu camu aren't fruiting, they are quite plain and thus when a bromeliad blooms it is quite surprising.

"Market Catfish." Within the photograph are stacked surubim or Amazonian catfish. Their designs are some of the most dramatic in the fish world of the Amazon, all save the peacock bass (tucunaré) and its impressive tailspots.

"Fruit Market." Bacuri palms produce a reddish-colored fruit (see photo). These fruits are often roasted and then eaten. Tucumã palms are tough since they are covered with long black spines. They flourish along the forest's edge.

"Pink River Dolphins" are also known as botos in Portuguese, while their counterparts are the grey river dolphins or tucuxis (pronounced took-ah-shes).

"Carrion Fish." The particular smell of the rancid boto must draw in the most paracatinga. I hope that this practice would be stopped immediately so that the pink river dolphins can survive in the wild.

"Opportunist." Forro is a sexy, two-step dance performed all over the Northeast.

"Water Monkey." The arawana is an amazing fish to watch hunt. They actually can jump over a meter out of the water to seize prey on trees. Their eyes are perfectly positioned to see better out of the water and to hone in on the targets. The story of them grabbing a baby sloth may be a bit overexaggerated, but it makes for lively debate. That would have to be the largest water monkey ever.

"Flat, Dry Ground Prone to Flood." The word "restinga" is actually pronounced "hestinga." Seringas are rubber-producing trees, while barrigudas (*Cavanillesia* *arborea*) have massive bottle-shaped trunks. Cheia translates to "floods" in Portuguese.

"Lily Trap." Amazonian lily flowers are adapted to trap scarab beetles in their flowers overnight. This guarantees pollination with other flowers on different plants. It is a unique evolutionary feature.

"Gas Bird." Hoatzin is pronounced "Wat-sin," thus the word play with "My dear Watson."

"Greater Tinamou." This is a bird often heard, but rarely seen in the Amazon. I have seen them though, but they are prized by hunters and, of course, by jaguars. Sucuriju is literally "big snake" or "big anaconda."

"Eatable Fear." It seems the majority of people I spoke to about the Amazon (and have never been there) are fearful of a great many diseases and dangers. There is little to fear if one is careful and takes proper precautions.

"Cemetery of the Caimans." The word "coureiros" comes from "couro" or leather. In some areas, the coureiros (pairs of hunters) stacked up carcasses by the hundreds. Today, caiman numbers have rebounded significantly, mostly due to protection and its status in CITES. The photograph for this poem comes from a black caiman that I believe was killed by villagers because it was getting too close to women who were washing clothes.

"Alarm Whistle." Capybaras, in the Pantanal, are very, very nervous. Of course, they are predated heavily by jaguars; therefore, they have adapted well. When there is a hint of danger, they make an alarm cough or whistle and they all jump into the nearest body of water and swim deep. This adaptation has allowed them to elude many predators. The youngest ones sometimes do not go into the water because they might be eaten by snakes or caiman.

"Tick, Tick." There are two meanings for "tiquetaque" in Portuguese: one is the noun "tick"; the other is the verb "to tick" to play off these concepts of parasitism and time. To be a good mother, she needs to teach her young that many species of birds can provide a service of removing the ticks. This is why it is key she is able to raise the youngster through the first two years. These are taught behaviors.

"Barren Tree." Chuva (shoe-va) is Portuguese for rain, while chusma (shoes-ma) means "crowd."

"The Magician." The parietal eye is a photoreceptor on the top of the iguana's head that can sense differences in light. Poaching in the Pantanal is actually decreasing, but it is still very difficult to see green iguanas in the wild. Perhaps in 10 years we will begin to see them recover to former numbers.

"Derelict Commune." The Xingu (Shin-goo) is a native culture comprised of 15 different tribes and 8 different languages.

Brambleby Books

**Rings in the Shingle –
Images and Poems from the
Norfolk Coast**
Stuart Medland
ISBN 978 1908241 160

**Norfolk Wildlife –
A Calendar and Site Guide**
Adrian M. Riley
ISBN 978 1908241 047

**British and Irish Butterflies
– The complete Field,
Identification and Site Guide
to the Species, Subspecies
and Forms**
Adrian M. Riley
ISBN 978 0955392 801

**Birds Words – Poetic images
of wild birds**
Hugh D. Loxdale
ISBN 978 0954334 734

**Arrivals and Rivals –
A duel for the winning bird**
Adrian M. Riley
ISBN 978 0954334 796

**Garden Photo Shoot –
A Photographer's Yearbook
of Garden Wildlife**
John Thurlbourn
ISBN 978 0955392 832

**Winging it –
Birding for Low-flyers**
Andrew Fallan
ISBN 978 0955392 856

**Never a dull Moment –
A naturalist's view of
British wildlife**
Ross Gardner
ISBN 978 0955392 870

**Buzzing!
Discover the poetry in
garden minibeasts**
Anneliese Emmans Dean
ISBN 978 1908241 078

**Birduder 344 –
A life list ordinary**
Rob Sawyer
ISBN 978 1908241 092

**And listen to the Waves –
Selected Poems**
Brian Churcher
ISBN 978 1908241 191

**Making Garden Meadows –
How to create a natural haven
for wildlife**
Jenny Steel
ISBN 978 1908241 221

**Sheer Cliffs and Shearwaters –
A Skomer Island Journal**
Richard Kipling
ISBN 978 1908241 214

www.ingramcontent.com/pod-product-compliance
Lightning Source LLC
Chambersburg PA
CBHW042129100526
44587CB00026B/4222